Spiritu
for the Everyday Christian

Walter Hilton and the 'Mixed Life'

Ian Bunting

GROVE BOOKS LIMITED
RIDLEY HALL RD CAMBRIDGE CB3 9HU

Contents

First Impression August 2024
ISSN 0262-799X
ISBN 978 1 78827 409 8

Introduction

1

Most people have had at least one experience in life which can only be described as 'out of this world.' Some may describe it as a 'fantasy,' upon which the human imagination makes play. For others it was 'a divine presence or absence,' or even 'an act of God,' whose meaning may be found through religious belief of one sort or another. Whether or not it happened in a religious setting, the experience defies attempts to describe it either in words or human logic.

Christians may wish to recapture such an experience of holy encounter with God, perhaps by going to church more faithfully, or by trying harder to believe, or by praying more fervently: all of which efforts often result in disappointment and failure. Historically, 'religion' is a word which derives from the Latin (*religio*) which means to 'get tethered.' It is certainly the way in which the church has tried to help people to recover, maintain and enrich a deep, life-giving and unifying Christian faith. In fourteenth-century England, which is the setting of this booklet, there was general agreement on the three essential foundations for a pursuit of realized holiness (apart, that is, from going to church): knowledge of the Bible; affection for Jesus in his humanity; and a focus on Christ's passion and the cross.

There was, however, a disturbing conflict of interest which continues to this day between the spirituality of Christians, individually or gathered together, and the doctrine, sacraments and practice of the wider church. In England in the fourteenth century this was played out in the sometimes uncertain relationship between mystically-inclined believers and the institutional church. But a profound cultural change was taking place. Religion was becoming both democratized and decentralized. How were the new mystics and their followers to relate to the church, its sacraments, rules and regulations?

How were the new mystics to relate to the church?

In the New Testament, Jesus notably describes his followers not as servants of God but as his 'friends' (John 15.15). Moreover, St Paul says to those in Rome, 'You are not in the flesh; you are in the Spirit, since the Spirit of God dwells in you' (Rom 8.9) and, still more controversially, he reminds members of the divided church in Corinth that 'you are God's temple...and God's Spirit dwells in you (1 Cor 3.16). For the Colossians he explains, it is 'this mystery, which is Christ in you, the hope of glory' (Col 1.27). From the beginning, therefore, the church has practised a personal faith, depending on the biblical account of Jesus, and regarding as essential: Christian commitment to the humanity of Jesus and the passion of Christ, albeit within the culture of the day.

The daily practice in a medieval community, and still the habit of many Catholic, Anglican and Protestant individuals today, was the *lectio divina*: First, read the Bible aloud (*lectio*). Secondly, using the imagination, learn and digest it inwardly by the heart (*meditatio*). Thirdly, respond individually with personal prayer for God's blessing (*oratio*). Fourthly, foretaste the hoped-for union with God, through contemplation (*contemplatio*).

In a nutshell the goal was, as St Paul put it, 'I want to know Christ and the power of his resurrection and the sharing of his sufferings by becoming like him in his death' (Phil 3.10). Among those who pursued this goal in England, one servant of the church was Walter Hilton who, like Martin Luther (1483–1546), was an Augustinian monk who deeply treasured the four gospels and the writings of St Paul. John Mark Comer (1980-), a present-day pastor, emphasizes the same priority, medium and message for the church in the twenty-first century: 'Find your inner monk…There's a monastic impulse of the Spirit in *all* of us, a part of our hearts that craves quiet prayer, solitude, and contemplation *and* that has a genuine desire (mixed with a tinge of healthy fear) for deep, vulnerable, heart-to-heart relationships with other followers of the Way.[1]

2

Hilton's 14th Century Context

The fourteenth century was an unlikely period of spiritual vitality when five English mystics, at least two of whom were women, began to exercise a remarkable influence. Nationally, it was marked by one disaster after another, beginning with a precarious monarchy pursuing the economically catastrophic Hundred Years War with France (1337–1453), which included two unprecedented poll taxes (1377 and 1379). A pandemic, the Black Death (1348–1357), halved the national population to about 3 million, causing an acute labour shortage in terms of supply and demand. The Peasants' Revolt (1381), a political, violent and grassroots reaction, was the unsurprising consequence.

The Church

Anti-clericalism was brewing in the nation, and the wider church suffered considerable reputational damage. Papal credibility and authority was weakened by the Great Schism (1378–1417). This divided Western Christendom following the election of two popes, one resident in Rome and the other in Avignon. Meanwhile, an increasing number of the middling sort of Englishmen were buying their freedom from serfdom, and proving to be increasingly independent and ambitious. They could not only read and write, but some were being drawn to the more individualistic and experiential type of religion practised by the mystics and the Lollards.[2]

Theological and religious conflict also mounted after John Wyclif (c 1330–1384) gained a following in the University of Oxford. He stirred academic and church opposition with his commitment to the final authority of the Scriptures, and their translation into the vernacular. He rejected not only the superstitious practices attaching to the doctrine of transubstantiation, but in about 1375 he wrote the revolutionary *De Dominio Divino.* This was soon being judged to have called into question the whole religious and political order of the day. In particular he taught God's immediate and unmediated lordship of every creature, on the basis not of the church's word but the Bible's.[3] In short, a succession of traumatic human events, each with consequences and serious implications for the populace at large, formed the backdrop to the political and theological change that would herald the English Reformation.

New Spiritual Vitality

Within the orthodox English Catholic church and from early in the previous thirteenth century the establishment of new monastic orders, the beginnings of women's public ministry, the promotion of crusades overseas, the building of churches, the development of the parish system and the evangelistic endeavours of the friars, all made an impact on the everyday life of English people. But more importantly, the emergence of a mystical and experiential spirituality that centred on the Holy Scriptures and the humanity and passion of Jesus Christ began to capture the public interest. It certainly caught the attention and commitment of individual Christians, whether living as hermits, or within a community, or in the mixed life of earnest lay Christians who wanted to know God.

Some of the writings of five English mystics have survived. They were not a single group, nor could any of them be defined as heretics, although that is how they were sometimes regarded because they believed and practised their faith in unconventional ways. What distinguished them was their prime concern for individuals, and their personal devotion to Jesus in his humanity and passion. For them, he was uniquely revealed in the Bible which was increasingly accessible to lay Christians in the vernacular.

Five English Mystics

In 1343 Richard Rolle (c 1300–1349), stated his positively affective (*cataphatic*) faith which became well-known. It was both personally and individually subjective, as well as introspectively sensitive. Towards the end of the century, however, a second, unknown author commended an experience, wholly different from Rolle's, of what God is not. The presence of God is devoid of all that can be felt or imagined (*apophatic*). A third mystic, Julian of Norwich (1342-c 1416), best known and most revered of the English mystics, in 1373 received sixteen 'showings' of God's motherly love in the person of Jesus, which is revealed through the *labour* of his crucifixion, and nurtured through the sacraments. Among her visitors was the emotionally and ecstatically charismatic Margery Kempe (1373-c 1438), known for her weeping. She prayed, 'Sovereign Christ Jesus, may my crying save as many people as have scorned me for it.'[4] She was wrongly suspected of being a Lollard.[5] Totally unlike these four, the fifth mystic, Walter Hilton (c 1343–1396), possibly attempted the solitary life before living in community. But if he did, he is remembered primarily as a spiritual director whose first surviving letters were addressed to a lay Christian who, in his mixed life, wanted to know God better.

3

The Spirituality of Walter Hilton

In about 1386 Walter Hilton became a monk of the Augustinian order at their house in Thurgarton, near Southwell in Nottinghamshire. The focus on Augustine's spiritual writings and biblical commentaries, together with the flexibility of their rule of life, meant that regular canons like Hilton could follow a mixed life that was both active in pastoral work and contemplative.[6] He summed up the context of his subsequent ministry: 'You will recognize that there are three manners of life: one is active, as in business; another is contemplative, as in spiritual service; and the third is made up of both, and so is called the mixed life.[7]

In two letters to a wealthy and leading layman, *To One New in Faith* and *On the Mixed Life*, Hilton demonstrated that he was a perceptive spiritual guide. He addressed 'a lord of worldly estate' and one 'new in faith' to encourage him in his desire to follow a more devotional plan of life. But the ultimate objective of all Christians is love for God, 'for love is properly a complete union of the lover and the beloved—one flesh; so God and a soul become, as it were, one in spirit. But such perfect union may not be realized in this life—only apprehended by desire and longing.'[8] He wanted everyday Christians to pursue a journey of faith. It would lead them from their first simple belief in God, hopefully accompanied by unselfish neighbourly behaviour, to heartfelt meditation on the humanity and passion of our Lord Jesus, and then on to a spiritual longing for 'heavenly joy and the endless bliss of God's presence.' Life rooted in a balanced threefold practice of charity, meditation and contemplation would lead, even one 'new in faith,' on a life-changing passage to spiritual enlightenment.

He wanted everyday Christians to pursue a journey of faith

As a tutor, Hilton proved himself to be a Bible-based and Christ-centred counsellor, committed to the formation of individual Christians. The goal should be a love for Jesus, who unites God and a human being in an intimate communion such as was modelled in the manhood of Jesus and the Passion of Christ. Selfish preoccupations, for instance an eye to one's own personal image or one's envy and anger directed against fellow-believers, are clearly unacceptable, along with covetousness and desire for 'creature comforts, food, or sexual pleasure.' But there are also acceptable if dangerous spiritual yearnings, for 'emotional or physical feeling, or any sensible sweetness of devotion, or special visions of angels or of the Lord in his earthly body.'[9]

In his later extensive advice to a reclusive anchorite (c 1394), in *The Scale of Perfection,* he builds on these warnings, emphasizing the threat of some of his contemporaries, possibly Lollards. In Hilton's view, they were tempted to shorten a lifetime journey of faith by focusing too much on intermediate blessings. Their unshakeable assurance of salvation, their personal spiritual inspiration, and their privately acquired convictions were examples. He concludes that such assurances can be no more than heretical presumptions, leading to fatal pride, exercise of unsanctified power and rejection of the church's doctrine and practice.

As a humble man, Hilton was willing to admit, 'Not that I have in feeling and in working what I have in saying…First I want to stir my own negligence in order to do better than I have done.'[10] Nonetheless, Hilton still speaks a word of encouragement to Christians today. In the gloomy shadow of our present circumstances, he reminds the church that it is possible for spiritual darkness to prove 'luminous,' and that leads on to a key question.

He reminds the church that it is possible for spiritual darkness to prove 'luminous,'

What is a Mystic?

The Greek *musterion*, to which the English word 'mystic' relates, means 'mystery' in the New Testament. It is much used by St Paul.[11] The earliest Christians understood that the knowledge of God in Christ surpasses the cognitive and intellectual human faculty, because it is spiritual and experiential and, above all, involves a relationship with the person of Jesus Christ recollected in his humanity and passion. From the early centuries of the church, some Christians retreated from everyday life to the life of a hermit (*eremite*), or of a monk living in a community (*coenobite*) to pursue this spiritual relationship. This enabled them to gain a heightened awareness of God's hidden presence by their reading of the Bible, by their personal commitment to the passionate Jesus of the New Testament, and by receiving the church's sacraments. The hope was that, in prayer and loving devotion, the Christian would advance through purification towards spiritual maturity by means of the practice of *meditation;* before progressing through illuminating *contemplation* to eventual *union* with God.

In the previous thirteenth century, a new spiritual climate had changed the practice of Christian devotion. It was not marked by any denial of the progressive aims of earlier Christian mystics. The Fourth Lateran Council (1215) had forbidden the formation of new religious orders. But it was at a time when the possibility of the development of new expressions of the Christian life, and how to live it out, were beginning to be recognized. As this happened, the wider church felt threatened by the unanswered questions posed by new communities. It could not be long before these issues would come to a head in controversy about what was sound evidence of the true church, and what must be eliminated as heresy. For instance, it was suspected by many that, in their practice of service to the community, active lay women were actually a threat both to ecclesiastical authority and the regular sacramental expectations of the church at large.[12]

For his part, Walter Hilton believed that the progression of holiness in the individual was also possible for the lay believer in the mixed life of the everyday Christian. But he insisted there was no shortcut to holiness. On reflection, and in his later writing on the subject, he concluded,

> A soul cannot suddenly jump from the lowest to the highest, any more than someone wanting to climb a high ladder and setting his foot on the lowest rung can next fly up to the highest. He needs to go gradually, one after another, until he can come to the top. It is just the same spiritually. Nobody is suddenly made perfect in grace, but through long exercise and skilled working a soul may come to it, especially when a wretched soul is taught and helped by him in whom lies all grace. For no soul can come to it without special help and inward teaching from him.[13]

Evelyn Underhill (1875–1941), editor of the Middle English version of *The Scale of Perfection* (1923), summarizing the calling of a medieval mystic believed: 'It is…the perfect flowering of that interior life of love and prayer to which in a greater or less degree every real Christian is called: and which it is the business of external religion to support and preserve.'[14]

A twentieth-century evangelical Christian, Aiden Wilson Tozer (1897–1963), wrote of the mystic,

> He differs from the ordinary orthodox Christian only because he experiences his faith down in the depths of his sentient being while the other does not. He exists in a world of spiritual reality. He is quietly, deeply, and sometimes almost ecstatically aware of the presence of God in his own nature and in the world around him. His religious experience is something elemental, as old as time and creation. It is immediate acquaintance with God by union with the eternal Son. It is to know that which passes knowledge.[15]

Tozer had detected among fellow Protestants an inadequate faith in which everything was made to centre upon the individual act of 'accepting Christ.' Thereafter, it seemed that Christians were not expected to crave any further revelation of God to their souls. In his view, they had been snared in the coils of the spurious logic which insists that if they have found Christ they need no more seek him.[16]

In the twenty-first century, a leading pastor, Timothy Keller (1950–2023), found the Scot John Murray (1898–1975) helpful in this regard:

> It is necessary for us to recognize that there is an intelligent mysticism in the life of faith...It must have the passion and warmth of love and communion because communion with God is the crown and apex of true religion.[17]

A contemporary Dominican spiritual director and interpreter of Hilton, Kevin Goodrich OP, offers us a hope and a promise:

> Mystical experience or saintliness is a grace, a free gift given by God to a human being. On the other hand, human beings can open themselves to God in ways that facilitate the gifting of mystical experience and saintly virtue.[18]

Bible-based

First and foremost, Walter Hilton meditated on the Scriptures. Among Christian historians of his period, none have assessed the contribution of Hilton more positively than the distinguished Roman Catholic historian Adrian Hastings (1929–2001). He concluded in a lecture in Southwell (1996) that the *Scale of Perfection* 'should probably be judged the most important and influential work of Catholic theology written in English in any century prior to 1500.'[19] He described Hilton's frequent use and insistence on Scripture as 'almost Wycliffite.' In common with Wyclif, and the Lollards, Hastings noted that the medieval mystics:

- Made ever-increasing use of English;
- Wrote for lay people;
- Made great use of the Scriptures;
- Believed in principle that the Bible should be available in English;
- Spoke of personal religion and 'the individual's direct experience of grace and God.'[20]

In counselling a layman to improve his mixed life, for instance, Hilton bases his advice on the gospel story where Jesus uses the example of Martha and Mary to make his point. Their two ways of caring for Jesus model the active and contemplative life, which Christians need to consider and adopt at appropriate times, and apply in different circumstances. In his own experience, Hilton knew two forms of the mixed life: first, that of a monk who like himself had both priestly and pastoral responsibilities which involved not a static but a travelling and many-faceted ministry; and secondly, that of his correspondent, a leading churchman in a secular vocation, in which as an everyday Christian he wants to grow in Christian devotion and maturity. While regarding both sorts as good Christians, he alerts the lay Christian to an important truth and accompanying danger: 'Understand that our Lord Jesus Christ is head of a spiritual body, the church. The limbs and members of its body are all Christian people.' Every member has an important part to play. But there will be a temptation for those living the mixed life to devote too much of their time to religious and spiritual activities. It can so preoccupy their minds that they neglect their Christian responsibilities for their neighbours, their fellow-workers, and an important facet of their own discipleship. If you fall for those temptations, he warns, 'You do no worship to God.'[21]

He may possibly have written this at the time, from his personal experience, when he was trying out the life of a hermit for himself. But a few years later, in writing to a reclusive anchoress, he repeats the same warning from his own mixed life as a circulating pastor. He turns to a gospel story to draw on the example of the risen Jesus who appeared to two disciples going home to their village, Emmaus. 'He opened the clearness of their wit, so that they could understand Holy Scripture.' And Hilton explains,

> ...how through the opening of the spiritual eye a soul receives a gracious love able to understand Holy Scripture, and how Jesus, who is hidden in Holy Scripture, shows himself to his lovers.

He adds,

> You must know that such gracious intuitions in Holy Scripture are nothing else but sweet letters, sent between a loving soul and Jesus the beloved: or else, if I am to speak more truthfully, between Jesus the true lover and the souls loved by him.'[22]

Interestingly, three twentieth-century Christian leaders have used a similar illustration. John Stott (1921–2011) wrote of the Scriptures as a love letter: 'So, too, we love the Bible because of Christ. It is his portrait. It is his love-letter.'[23] David Watson (1933–1984) also explained how his view changed after he had been 'filled with the Spirit' in 1963: 'I read the Bible as never before, and certain passages leapt out at me as though they were alive. They all seemed like love-letters from God.'[24] Former Archbishop, Rowan Williams (1950-), wrote of the Bible as a book to be inhabited:

> Reading the Bible is about listening to God in Jesus...It is letting the Holy Spirit bring you inside the story of how God related to the ancient Israelites and the first Christian believers—letting the Holy Spirit bring you inside that story so that you recognize it as *your* story.[25]

For Reflection

- How do you inhabit the Bible today?

Christ-centred

Secondly, Walter Hilton was devoted to the person of Jesus. In outlining the mixed life to his correspondent, he offers this advice: Having reflected on 'your own past sins and the frailties to which you are prone...Also you must properly have in mind the humanity of our Lord.'[26] Here, he addresses a leading layman, educated and with some understanding of the Holy Scriptures but new in faith, and in whom Hilton expects a deeper consciousness of God, than he does in those he describes as the 'unlettered,' 'who should concentrate more on external deeds to his Christian brethren, so to kindle the fire, thus exercising the love of God for them.'[27] But in both he anticipates meditation on the humanity of Jesus which 'wisely pursued, nourishes our desire for God.'[28] All progression of the individual Christian will be in the spirit of the living Christ, present in the believer. The assurance of salvation and the experience of the ongoing love of Jesus is the gift of the Holy Spirit, as Hilton understands it.[29] We owe all creation to God the Father, and our human life to his sovereign will. But we find our wisdom in his Son, and receive our forgiveness, conversion and full redemption through his love.

St Paul makes this plain in the core of his own personal faith: 'I decided to know nothing among you except Jesus Christ, and him crucified' (1 Cor 2.2). Only by such a personal identification with Jesus in his humanity and passion is it possible for Paul to go on to preach about the divinity and power of Christ, and claim it displays the endless wisdom of God. Hilton sees it as a twofold process. First, '*How everyone can be saved by the passion of Christ if he asks, however wretched he may be.*' For sin is a spiritual sickness and, 'this name Jesus in English is nothing else but *healer* or *health*.'[30] But Hilton goes on to sum up the practical benefit the Christian derives from meditating on his passion. Secondly, it addresses the much deeper weight for humankind, the ongoing temptation to sin.

> It may be called the carnal love of God, as St Bernard calls it, inasmuch as it is set in the human nature of Christ. It is very good, and a great help in destroying great sins, and a way to come to virtues, and so afterward into contemplation of the divine nature. For a person shall not commonly come to spiritual delight in the contemplation of Christ's divinity unless he first comes in imagination, by anguish and compassion for his humanity.[31]

In short, Hilton speaks of the 'delight' of the believer in contemplating Christ's passion. Moreover, there is a further priceless spiritual benefit. Christians from the start will find help coming to them in the ongoing spiritual perils and temptations which threaten them as they progress in their Christian experience. Here lies the central life-changing spiritual insight which Hilton has experienced for himself, and wants to share. It continues to be the very ground upon which Christians should walk every day, and the secret of keeping them on the right path. Let the words of Hilton speak for themselves: .

> Now since you are on the sure way, if you want to speed on your travels and make a good journey each day, you should hold these two things often in your mind—humility and love. That is: *I am nothing; I have nothing; I desire only one thing*...Humility says, I am nothing; I have nothing. Love says, I desire only one thing, and that is Jesus. These two strings, well-fastened with mindfulness of Jesus, make good harmony on the harp of the soul when they are skilfully touched with the finger of reason. For the lower you strike upon the one, the higher sounds the other; the less you feel that you are, or that you have of yourself through humility, the more you long to have of Jesus in the desire of love.[32]

For Reflection

- How do you personally contemplate both Christ's 'humanity' and his 'passion'?

4 Hilton's Three Steps to Perfection

In his two letters to one 'new in faith,' Walter Hilton prescribes a 'contemplative quality of life' which will lead him in three stages as, 'little by little and by degrees he grows in grace toward the perfection he seeks.'[33] He likens the needed process to lighting a fire, which starts as a small flickering coal in the soul. First, add some 'sticks of wood.' If it does not then begin to burn brighter, blow on it by going alone to 'your prayer and meditation.' 'Holding your good labours of the active life as nothing in your own sight, and valuable only in his mercy, be meekly aware of your own wretchedness and frailties, and attribute all your good efforts sincerely to him.'[34]

For a person Hilton describes as 'educated,' it will be good to gather 'sticks from Holy Scripture and so nourish that fire.' For those who are 'unlettered' and have no Scriptures and commentaries to hand he counsels, more 'external deeds to their Christian companions.' He adds that Scripture says, 'Our God is a consuming fire.' (Heb 12.29; Deut 4.24). God's purpose is therefore that 'this fire should be recognized, preserved, and strengthened, for it is sent for our salvation. The more desire that you have toward him, the more is this love within you.'[35] Hilton wrote of three stages of Christian faith and practice as the outward evidence of spiritual progress.

The first stage of this 'fire of love' is visible in humble, ordinary good works. For his correspondent, this will be resourced by Scripture reading and instruction, accompanied and enriched by personal prayer and meditation.

The second stage will be marked by a heartfelt loathing of the pleasures of this world, a longing for life with a clear conscience in God's presence, and the 'desire' for it will be exhibited in effective Christian action, while at the same time enjoying a taste for spiritual things. Godly desire will be nourished by:

- Reflecting on one's past sins and ongoing frailties;
- Meditating on the humanity of Jesus and his passion;
- Developing the fruit of the Spirit;
- Recalling the 'saints of our Lord.'[36]

In the third stage, Hilton envisages an even higher hope for the lay Christian's mixed life. Referring to the view of St Augustine that 'the life of each Christian is a continual expression of desire toward God,' he writes, 'Contemplation should be an object of our desire.'[37] He should 'not seek after any emotional or physical feeling, nor any sensible sweetness of devotion, nor special visions of angels or the Lord in his earthly body, for these are not actually such a great matter.'[38] But the desire for God is only a beginning. A taste of love is not the love of God.

> For love is properly a complete union of the lover and the beloved—one flesh; so God and a soul become, as it were, one in spirit. But such perfect union may not be realized in this life—only apprehended by desire and longing…It is by the gift of this implanted desire that we may be saved, for it is an expression of love unto him such as we can have in our present condition.[39]

To be sure, Hilton envisaged a progression from the practically expressed faith of the everyday Christian, to a personal belief in and love for Jesus which is accompanied by the desire for a spiritual apprehension of the Godhead itself. This is the height of love, and the final goal and fullness of joy for the human soul.

It is in the perception of these three stages and his commitment to reaching the summit of contemplation that Hilton shows himself to be a true mystic. He seeks to foster an understanding of the ineffable nature of God's loving presence in one 'new in faith,' and issues a warning about settling for a secondary blessing. 'Do not hang excessively long upon a moment of spiritual intensity,' or be 'gaping after some peculiar stirring or wondrous feeling.'[40] A few years later, in his last recorded message to the anchoress, Hilton concludes, 'All this loving courtship and private talk between Jesus and a soul may be called a hidden word, of which Holy Scripture says, "Now a word came stealing to me, my ear received the whisper of it"' (Job 4.12).[41] His first two letters end with the wise observation of St Gregory (c 540–604) who said, 'No one is suddenly made sovereign in grace, but little by little one begins, and by degrees grows in grace toward the perfection which is sought.'[42]

Kevin Goodrich OP urges Christians today to attend to 'the fire of their faith' and concludes: 'One of the best things Christian workers of all kinds can do for the people they serve is to attend to the fire of their own faith.'[43]

For Reflection

- How far up are you on the ladder to perfection? How do you fuel 'the fire of your faith'?

Luminous Darkness

Walter Hilton was well aware from his own experience that the practice of contemplation calls for 'special purity...which may not be had without both great exercise of the body and continual travail of the spirit, in devout prayer, fervent desire and meditation.'[44] The way forward involves brutal self-knowledge, a concentration on the humanity and passion of Jesus, and quite possibly a spiritual experience that St John of the Cross (1542–1591) was later to call, 'the dark night of the soul.' Hilton saw it in a good light:

> Certainly, I would rather feel and have a true desire and a pure longing in my heart for my Lord Jesus, even though I should see nothing of him at all with my spiritual eye, than have without this desire all the bodily penance of all men alive, all visions or revelations of angels appearing, songs and sounds, savours or smells, burnings and delights felt by the body—in short, all the joys of heaven and earth which I could have without this desire toward my Lord Jesus.[45]

The reason he adds this caution is because he detects a danger of seeking and resting in some experiences which appear to be spiritual but are not necessarily so. Such experiences were not uncommon among the Lollards who Hilton judges to be heretics, posing a threat to the established church and Roman Catholic doctrine and practice to which he is deeply committed. More importantly, they could be evidence of false light. As for himself: 'It sufficeth to me for to live in truth principally, and not in feeling.'[46]

Later he foretells a particular problem in this regard for the anchoress he is counselling. He tells her she is in danger of falling for a dangerous inner temptation, which he describes as 'wicked stirrings and painful vexations that befall the heart from the world, the flesh and the devil.' He explains that when we love God and our brothers and sisters we will live wholly in the light, and will perceive the loves of this world to be false light which 'does not perform what it promises' (1 John 2.9–10). For the present therefore, we have to 'abide awhile in the night' because we cannot come suddenly from love for the world to a perfect love of God. 'But this is a good night and a luminous darkness, for it is a shutting out of the false love of this world, and it is a drawing nearer to the true day.' Yes, it can prove to be either a painful or a restful darkness but, if accompanied by a grace-given desire to have the love of Jesus, it is a darkness which drives worldly and carnal affections out of the soul and 'brings it into this rich nothing.'[47] Such a strange and alien but memorable and seemingly countercultural richness lies in the depth of her longing for the presence of Jesus.

For it happens to him as if someone has been a great while in the sun and afterward comes suddenly into a dark house where no sun shines. At first he shall be as if blind, seeing nothing at all, but if he will wait awhile he shall soon be able to see around him: first large things and then small ones, and later all that is in the house. It is just the same spiritually.[48]

For Reflection

- The poet Edwin Muir wrote, 'Strange blessings never in Paradise / Fall from these beclouded skies.'[49] How far does your desire for God illuminate your dark times?

Midday Devil

In his second address to the anchoress, which can be described as a summing-up of all that he has to say both in the mixed life and in the scale of perfection, Walter Hilton introduces a shadowy figure in the Bible. Like Satan, he 'disguises himself as an angel of light' (2 Cor 11.14) and in the Middle Ages was linked to the one identified by the psalmist, who wreaks 'destruction that wastes at noonday' (Ps 91.6). The 'Midday Devil,' or the 'Noonday Demon,' as described by the Desert Fathers in the fourth and fifth centuries and then by St Benedict (480–547), was regarded as a dangerous threat to Christians who dedicate their lives to a religious calling whether in community or as a hermit. The problem was revealed in the not uncommon temptation of the dedicated monk or nun to surrender either to a weary slothfulness on the one hand, or to meaningless activity on the other. These aberrations were considered at that time to be sure evidence of an unacknowledged temptation to give up on the religious life. Evidence of the Midday Devil's success in this regard could be gauged by the resulting *acedia,* literally 'lack of care,' or as it is more generally understood today, 'depression.'

Doubtless, Hilton knew this when he warned the reclusive anchoress in her lonely cell of one of whom she should be beware. But to this he contributed his own unique perspective on another problem for Christians both then and now. Whether or not it was with the Lollards in mind or seemingly emotionally enthusiastic men and women like Richard Rolle and Margery Kempe, he alerted his correspondent to another tactic of the Midday Devil. He could appear in the form of a religious imposter who, in effect, promoted a spiritual presumption, which could have dire consequences for the English church, both in its doctrine and practice.

What Hilton found spiritually lacking in the lives of those he criticized here was a perceptive appreciation of the depth and ongoing nature of enduring sin within individual Christians. This could lead them to overconfidence and a presumption in which they judged each other. Consequently, he signals the danger of what he describes as the 'light of knowledge,' professed by some of his contemporaries. This can and does sometimes appear between what he likens to two black rainy clouds. He explains, 'The upper cloud is presumption and exaltation of the self; the lower cloud is the abasement and humiliation of his fellow Christian.' He explains that,

> The words they sow by preaching tend to backbiting, strife and the making of discord, and to the condemnation of certain classes and people, and yet they say that all this is charity and zeal for righteousness. But that is not true...[50]

What Hilton wants Christians to recognize is that those who want to forsake love of the world and to come to the true love of God must appreciate more than the luminous darkness in which they first came face to face with their own sinful selves before they were graciously illumined by Jesus Christ. They are now in danger of falling for the error of overlooking the continuing darkness of their own inner nature. They may now refuse to acknowledge both what they were before their illumination, and forget about the essential, ongoing and needed 'luminous darkness' until their love for God is perfect, which is not possible in this life. The fact is that Christians go on displaying 'envy and quarrelling' which is 'earthly, bestial and devilish.'

> And so by these tokens—which are pride, presumption, disobedience, disdain, backbiting and other such sins (for these follow later)—may the feigned light be known from the true. For the true sun does not show himself by special visitation to give light of understanding or perfect charity to a soul, unless the firmament is first made bright and clear of clouds; that is, unless the conscience is made clean by the fire of burning desire for Jesus in this darkness, which lays waste and burns all wicked stirrings of pride, vainglory, wrath, envy, and all other sins of the soul, as the prophet says: 'Fire goes before him, and consumes his adversaries on every side' (Ps 97.3).[51]

For Reflection

- How does the Midday Devil threaten your own spiritual growth and maturity?

Ultimate Goal

Through contemplation on the humanity and passion of Jesus, Walter Hilton wants his readers to reach the ultimate goal of a perfect and personal union with God in Christ. It is a target impossible to achieve by any human being in this world. Nevertheless, we are to stretch for it, and he does his utmost to show those he is counselling that it is possible for a Christian to do that, even one in the mixed life of a powerful lay churchman, or a pastorally-committed monk in a community like himself, or the reclusive anchoress whom he addresses in his last surviving communication.

Yet, the most we can reach in this life is only a taste of perfection in our relationship with God. And to be sure, that will depend on what we understand by contemplation, and how we go about it. Along with St Paul, Hilton uses an everyday and helpful illustration when he likens the human soul to a mirror in which Christians see both themselves and God. 'All of us, with unveiled faces, seeing the glory of the Lord as though reflected in a mirror, are being transformed into the same image from one degree of glory to another, for this comes from the Lord, the Spirit' (2 Cor 3.18).

Hilton therefore urges us to remember that the imagined mirror must be kept bright, clean and above all preserved from our self-centred efforts to see in it a bodily figure with its five senses, and the best possible picture of ourselves. When it comes to Hilton's view of contemplation, it is best to let Hilton speak for himself:

> It is very hard, for a soul is rough and much in the flesh, to have sight and knowledge of itself, or of an angel or of God: it falls at once into imagination of a bodily shape, and supposes by that to have the sight of itself, and so of God, and so of spiritual things; and that cannot be. For all spiritual things are seen and known by the understanding of the soul, not by imagination.[52]

If one is to see a clear image both of oneself and of the Lord Jesus, there is therefore a danger of putting too much confidence in appearances defined by our religious experiences among which, as already noted, he lists 'great fervours and much sweetness in devotion.' Whether or not Hilton had Richard Rolle, Margery Kempe or the Lollards in mind, he believed such feelings could be deceptive devotional excesses that were no more than the outcome of the 'imagination and not in understanding.' He concluded that such a believer, 'has not yet come to perfect love or to contemplation.' He then sums up his mature reflection on how God makes himself known to a Christian. He does it little by little

> ...not blindly, nakedly and without savour, as with a scholar who sees him by his learning, only through the power of his naked reason; but he sees him through an understanding which is strengthened and illuminated by the gift of the Holy Spirit, with a wonderful reverence and a secret burning love, and with spiritual savour and heavenly delight more clearly and fully than it may be written or told.[53]

Hilton did not rubbish out of hand the faith, practices and experiences of believers as they progress through the three degrees of a growing love for God. 'All are good, but each one is better than another.'[54] Nevertheless, the best model of a contemplative in the Bible is Mary Magdalene in her meeting with the risen Christ. She was rebuked by the one she loved, for her bodily rather than spiritual devotion when she desired to hold on to him after he rose from the grave (John 20.17). Hilton had earlier explained why this was so to one 'new in faith':

> You ought to be thinking of the soul of our Lord Jesus. It is he who was fully joined to the Godhead, passing beyond comparison our Lady and all other creatures. For in the person of our Lord are two natures: that is God and man, fully joined...as the apostle says, 'For in him dwelt all the fullness of the Godhead bodily' (Col 2.9).

In meditating on the humanity and passion of Jesus, Hilton says the Christian finds not only personal comfort but also God's presence among us. The point he is making is both subtle and profound. As we contemplate the soul of Jesus we will also have in mind the power, the wisdom, and the goodness of our Lord made known in all his creatures. 'For although we may not see God himself here living among us, we may behold him, love him, and fear him, marvelling in his power, wisdom, and goodness as we see these revealed in his works and his creatures.'[55]

For Reflection

- How do you recognize and contemplate the presence of God in your world today?

The Mixed Life in Practice

In brief and in his correspondence with one new in faith and the reclusive anchoress, Walter Hilton calls for evidence of three key aspirations:

- Heartfelt 'desire' for a loving union with God;
- Bible-based 'meditation' on the humanity and passion of Jesus;

- Composed 'contemplation' on our ultimate union with God, through Jesus.

Therefore:

Nurture a Desire to Know God, and Settle for Nothing Less

The 'good labours of the active life' will be evidence of the 'desire' to be saved which God has graciously planted in us, but also an expression of a 'desire' to love God.

> We are working to counter sins of the world and illicit pleasures with our desire of him and his goodness, allowing all things that would hinder us in our coming to him to be burned up in the desire of him which he has planted in us.'[56]

The 'unlettered' believer 'will concentrate more on external deeds to his Christian brethren, so to kindle the fire, thus exercising the love of God for them.'[57] For the anchoress he uses a different illustrative example.

> For Christ is the door, and he is the porter; and without his leave and his livery no one can come in there, as he says himself: No one comes to the Father but by me. That is to say: Nobody can come to the contemplation of the Deity unless by the fullness of humility and charity he is first reformed to the likeness of Jesus in his manhood.[58]

Hilton therefore expects of the reformed believer, 'new in faith,' a credible witness that will be self-evident in a changed life. In the case of 'unlettered' believers, he assures them: 'Your action exhibits your desire,' and: 'Your action speaks for itself.'[59] But he repeats this advice later for the benefit of the better educated, using the different but apposite illustration of the uniform Christians are called to wear. 'For this reason, prepare yourself to put on his likeness—that is, the humility and charity which are his livery—and then he will want to know you familiarly and show you his mystery.'[60]

Practise Bible-based Meditation on the Humanity and Passion of Jesus

Hilton believes such meditation will stir the Christian's affection to a greater love for Jesus. However, while emphasizing the need for it, he warns against excessive emphasis on the wish for a particular religious experience or moment. 'Do not allow your heart to dally too long in this wish, as if you were expecting or even gaping after some peculiar stirring or wondrous feeling, other than the sort you have already had.'[61] As noted above, he said more on the subject of meditation in writing later to the anchoress.

> When the remembrance of Christ's passion or any point of his humanity is thus caused in your heart by such spiritual vision, with devout affection answering to it—then, know well that it is not your own doing, neither the pretence of any wicked spirit, but by the grace of the Holy Spirit. For it is an opening of the eye of the spirit into Christ's humanity...[62]

'Contemplation Should Be an Object of Our Desire, and Works of Our Active Life Pursued Without Anger or Undue Coercion'[63]

Hilton illustrates all that he has to say on the subject of reforming a soul (including contemplation) with the example of three persons standing in the light of the sun. The first is blind. The second has eyes shut. The third is clear-sighted. The blind man has to be told that he is standing in the sun and is reformed because he believes in God and what the church teaches him. It is sufficient for salvation. The second man with his eyes shut sees a great light only through his closed eyelids. He is contemplative in that he sees something of the divinity of Jesus, reformed in faith and in feeling, and enjoys a partial but convincing sight of supreme goodness and a blessed life in Jesus. The third man does not need to believe, because 'he openly sees the face of Jesus in the glory of heaven, where there is no faith; and therefore he is fully reformed in feeling.'[64]

Pete Greig (1968-), founder of the *24–7 Prayer Movement*, has taught on prayer for more than twenty-five years. Perhaps appealing particularly to Christians of Generation Z (born between 1995 and 2009), he writes,

> Sometimes it's possible to become so absorbed in God's reality that I forget myself completely. I am no longer consciously praying or worshipping. Words would be inadequate and even inappropriate. It's as though time has stopped and I've somehow stepped into eternity...

He goes on to encourage everyday Christians to make the same discovery with the help of an odd but illuminating illustration from our enthralment to modern media.

> You may be surprised to learn that you probably embark upon precisely this kind of meditative and contemplative journey every time you go to the cinema. First, at the start of the movie, it's 'you and the film.' You are eating popcorn, working hard to pay attention...But then, if the film is good, it starts to affect you. It draws you in. You laugh and cry. You find yourself caring about the characters, forgetting that they are actors. You no longer need to work at getting into the film because the film is getting into you. Meditation has turned into contemplation.[65]

5

Conclusion

Walter Hilton was a perceptive spiritual director within the medieval English Catholic church who wanted everyday Christians to pursue a pilgrimage that leads from basic faith, belief in God accompanied by unselfish behaviour, to a heartfelt desire and affection for Jesus Christ of the gospels. Founded on this lifelong passion, 'meditation' will lead even one 'new in faith' on a life-changing journey to spiritual enlightenment. Hilton may therefore be reckoned as a proto-evangelical English Catholic, inasmuch as he was a biblically-based and Christ-centred counsellor, and committed to enabling the spiritual formation of individual Christians within the established church of his day.

Walter Hilton still speaks today to all evangelical Catholics, Orthodox, Protestants and independents. He reminds us of the timeless loving purpose of the ever-loving God who is now and finally revealed to humankind in the person of one known to Hilton simply as the 'Lord Jesus.' Although he was particularly critical of those he considered to be anti-Catholic, certainly not all the independently minded and Lollard followers of Wyclif deserved Hilton's fiercely outspoken condemnation. Yet, when seen today from a contemporary perspective, even Hilton's bitter critique of some evangelical Christians as he encountered them in his own day can be seen in a useful light. His is a much-needed indictment of religious hypocrisy, presumption, triumphalism and the abuse of power wherever and whenever it appears in the church.

Hilton believed in a Bible-based and Christ-centred relationship with God-in-person, focused on the incarnate, crucified and resurrected Jesus, and the ongoing work of his Holy Spirit in the life of the Christian. He commended the reforming work of God to be found in a life-long pilgrimage of increasing holiness, overcoming the 'midday devil' and guided by God even where it is experienced within a 'luminous darkness.' The journey will continue for the believer to its end in a 'perfection' which is the vision of God. In sum, the unmistakable goal of Walter Hilton in his surviving writings is the renewal of the individual as a contribution to the renewal of the church.

Primary Sources

The Scale of Perfection. From ten manuscript sources, in Middle English, transcribed by D Inward, with an introduction by E Underhill (London: John M Watkins, 1923).

Toward a Perfect Love: The Spiritual Counsel of Walter Hilton, translated into modern English with an introduction by D L Jeffrey (Portland, OR: Multnomah Press, 1985).[66]

Walter Hilton: The Scale of Perfection, John P H Clark and R Dorward (trans and eds) (New York: Paulist Press, 1991).

Notes

1 J M Comer, *Practicing the Way: Be with Jesus, Become Like Him, Do as He Did* (London: SPCK, 2024) pp 202–203.

2 Followers of John Wyclif, who denied transubstantiation, read the first English translation of the Bible (c 1390) and argued for a return to the pure and apostolic church. 'Lollard' was their nickname.

3 R L Pole (ed), *Iohannis Wycliffe: De Dominio Divino Libri Tres*, Cap V (London: Wyclif Society, 1890) p 33.

4 *The Book of Margery Kempe,* T T Triggs (trans) (Tunbridge Wells: Burns and Oates, 1995). Cited in G L Miller, *The Way of the English Mystics* (Tunbridge Wells: Burns and Oates, 1996) p 130.

5 Her parish priest at St Margaret's, Kings Lynn, was William Sawtrey who was the first Lollard martyr to be burned after the passing of *De haeretico comburendo* in 1401.

6 Walter Hilton, *Toward a Perfect Love,* D L Jeffrey (trans) (Portland, OR: Multnoma Press, 1985) pp 3–34.

7 *Mixed Life*, II.iii.

8 *Mixed Life*, II.xvi.

9 *Mixed Life*, II.xv.

10 J P H Clark and R Dorward, *Walter Hilton: The Scale of Perfection* (Mahwah, NJ: Paulist Press, 1991) p 160. *The Scale*, I:92.

11 *musterion:* 'The secret thoughts, plans and dispensations of God which are hidden from the human reason, as well as from all other comprehension below the divine level, hence must be revealed to those for whom it is intended.' W F Arndt and F W Gingrich, *A Greek-English Lexicon of the New Testament* (Cambridge University Press, 1957) p 532.

12 Margaret Portete was burned in 1310, principally for writing her book, *The Mirror of Simple Souls*, in her native French. This, in a period when communities of the 'free spirit' sprang up on the Continent with 'a belief in the presence of God in the human soul via the Holy Spirit and the need to work out a grassroots salvation of mankind individually.' R E Learner, *The Heresy of the Free Spirit in the Later Middle Ages* (Notre Dame, IN: University of Notre Dame Press, 1991).

13 *The Scale*, II.17. *The Scale of Perfection*, edited from MST Sources, with an introduction by E Underhill, (London: John M Watkins, 1923) pp 288–289.

14 *ibid*, p xxxi.

15 A W Tozer, *The Christian Book of Mystical Verse* (Harrisburg, PA: Christian Publications, 1963) p vi.

16 AW Tozer, *The Pursuit of God* (Harrisburg, PA: Christian Publications, 1948) p 15.

17 J Murray, *Redemption: Accomplished and Applied* (Grand Rapids, MI: Eerdmans, 1955) pp 169–170. Cited in T Keller, *Prayer: Experiencing Awe and Intimacy with God* (London: Hodder and Stoughton, 2014) p 16.

18 K Goodrich OP, *Mystic Bonfires: Walter Hilton and the Development of Practical Spiritual Theology* (Eugene, OR: Wipf and Stock, 2022) pp 20–21.

19 A Hastings, *Walter Hilton*, 8th Southwell Lecture, 17 October 1996 (Diocese of Southwell and Nottingham: Southwell Minster, NG25 0JL, 1996) p 9.

20 *ibid*, p 7.

21 *Mixed Life*, II.viii.

22 *The Scale*, II:43.

23 J Stott, *Fundamentalism and Evangelism* (London: Crusade Booklets, 1956) p 22.

24 D Watson, *You are My God* (London: Hodder and Stoughton, 1983) p 56.

25 R Williams, *Being Christian: Baptism, Bible, Eucharist, Prayer* (London: SPCK, 2014) p 36.

26 *Mixed Life,* II.xix and xx.

27 *Mixed Life*, II.xiii.

28 *Mixed Life*, II.xx.

29 *The Scale,* II.34.

30 *The Scale,* I:44.

31 *The Scale,* I:35.

32 *The Scale,* II.21.

33 *Mixed Life*, II.xxviii.

34 *Mixed Life*, II:xiii.

35 *Mixed Life*, II.xiv.

36 *Mixed Life*, II.xviii-xxii.

37 *Mixed Life*, II.xi.

38 *Mixed Life*, II.xv.

39 *Mixed Life*, II.xvi.

40 *Mixed Life*, II.xxvii–xxviii.

41 *The Scale* II:46.

42 *Mixed Life*, II.xvii–xviii.

43 K Goodrich OP, *Mystic Bonfires, op cit,* p 35.

44 *Mixed Life*, II.iii.

45 *The Scale,* I:47.

46 H Pepwell, *The Song of Angels* (1521). In Edmund Gardner, *The Cell of Self-knowledge*, New Mediaeval Library, 1910, p 73. Cited in *The Scale of Perfection, op cit,* p xxiii.

47 *The Scale,* ii.24.

48 *The Scale*, II.27.

49 Edwin Muir (1887–1959), 'One Foot in Eden,' *Collected Poems* (London: Faber and Faber, 1960) p 227.

50 *The Scale*, II.26.

51 *The Scale*, II.26.

52 *The Scale,* II.30.

53 *The Scale,* II.32.

54 *The Scale*, II.30.

55 *Mixed Life*, II.xxii.

56 *Mixed Life*, II.xvi.

57 *Mixed Life*, II.xiii.

58 *The Scale*, I.91.

59 *Mixed Life*, II.xvii.

60 *The Scale,* I.51, 'Livery' is the clothing that distinguished the servant of a noble person. Interestingly, Hugh Latimer (1485–1555) used the same image in a sermon in Grimsthorpe, 28 October 1552, 'So our Saviour, which is the Lord above all lords, would his servants to be known by their liveries and badge, which badge is love.' *Sermons of Latimer*, Parker Society (Cambridge University Press, 1844) p 448.

61 *Mixed Life*, II.xviii.

62 *The Scale*, I:35.

63 *Mixed Life*, II.xi.

64 *The Scale*, II.32.

65 P Greig, *How to Pray: A Simple Guide for Normal People* (London: Hodder and Stoughton, 2019) p 130.

66 Originally 'Letters to a Layman' and called *Epistle on the Medled Life* or *Epistle on the Mixed Life.* This work is derived from the MST transcription by Horstmann of Bodleian MST Vernon.